Meeting Jazzy

To Mum and Dad

I love you always

Meeting Jazzy: Making friends with a dog
Author – Cathy Ewald

© Cathy Ewald 2021 (text)
© Honey Randall 2021 (illustrations)

www.jazzydoodie.com.au
contact@jazzydoodie.com.au

The moral rights of the author and the illustrator have been asserted.
All rights reserved. No part of this book may be reproduced in whole or part, stored, posted on the internet, or transmitted in any form or by any means, electronic, mechanical, photocopying, recording, or other, without written permission from the author.

Illustrations by Honey Randall
Editing, design and publishing support by www.AuthorSupportServices.com

ISBN: 9781922375056 Pbk

A catalogue record for this book is available from the National Library of Australia

Hi! I'm Jazzy Doodie the dog.
I like to meet new friends at the park
But if you frighten me, I might bark.

I don't think the same way as you
I can hear and smell more, it's true.

I'm a dog, not a toy

Let's find some games we can both enjoy!

I can feel happy or sad

Like you, I can be scared, angry or glad.

So, don't pull my tail or tug at my ears
Like you, I have some fears.

How do you make friends with me?
I like girls and boys to be gentle, you see.

Ask my mum if you want to give me a pat
I might want to play, or just rest on my mat.

I like to sniff sniff, one two
To check the smell of you.

Don't put your hand over my head
Let me walk away if I go to my bed.

Pat me on my back or my chest

That's what I like the best.

I use my body instead of words
I don't sing like the birds.

Look at my tail and look at my ears
If they go down, I am showing my fears.

If I am panting and it's not hot
I might be a bit worried or maybe a lot.

Now when you are out and see me
You know how we can play happily.
I'm Jazzy! Let's be friends!

About the Author

CATHY EWALD is a computer geek who loves dogs and lives with two of them, Jazzy Doodie herself and new friend Lulu.

After Jazzy Doodie came to live with Cathy, she realised that kids and dogs need to learn how to be friends. Lots of books have been written about training dogs, but not so many about teaching young people how dogs communicate so she decided to do something about it.

You can find out more about Cathy and Jazzy at www.jazzydoodie.com.au

About the Illustrator

HONEY RANDALL is a Queensland girl through and through, and has lived in several locations around the Sunshine State. She enjoys drawing and writing, and works mostly digitally with the occasional piece using traditional pencils and pens.

Find more of her work at @honey_elizabeth_illustration on instagram